LIFE RELATED TRUTH

PRATIBHA CHAUREL

Contents

Contents

ONE

"Promises are meant to be broken"

People always say this line

"Then the one who keep their promises, are they fools?"

No they are loyal

And make promises doesn't mean to break it,

It means to carry on, but

The people surrounding you can break it easily

Because they don't care about you and anyone's feeling.

-**Pratibha chaurel**

ꝐꝐꝐ

"Don't do anything for those who think you are not capable,

But win the whole world for those who think you are capable and achieve lots of thing in life."

Pratibha Chaurel

ꝐꝐꝐ

"You know your talent and your worth,

People makes fun of you because they don't know it,

Then

Why you always proof yourself in front of these types of people,

Right and good people respect your talent,

Wrong and bad people disrespect your talent,

Show your talent but in right places."
Pratibha Chaurel

ᑭᑭᑭ

"Life becomes fulfilling when
You realize there is no one who makes you happy,
So be happy yourself."
Pratibha chaurel

TWO

"If any human always smile and talk, then it doesn't mean that they

have no problem in life."

Pratibha Chaurel

ꝒꝒꝒ

"In Life there is three types of people you always meet

Shy and Silent

Open minded and talkative

Silent and open both , its depend on their mood."

Pratibha chaurel

ꝒꝒꝒ

"Respect yourself first what you are,

because if you don't respect yourself then no one respect you,

And that is the reality of life."

Pratibha Chaurel

ꝒꝒꝒ

"Some people can't change their perception about you,

So don't waste your time to change their perception about you,

Just focus on your goals."

Pratibha Chaurel

THREE

"If you have different opinion, different thoughts and unique personality

than it okk,because unique things have their own name and fame, not the same as all have."

Pratibha Chaurel

"Those people who don't know how to laugh out loud,

cannot live the freely life."

Pratibha Chaurel

"Light walks into life like Silver Lining."

Pratibha Chaurel

"Society always gives you knowledge and advices, but

If you are right then you do not need to listen to anyone, keep moving forward in your life."

Pratibha Chaurel

FOUR

"It is a good thing to think of others as big and wise, but it is wrong to not think of yourself as anything."

Pratibha Chaurel

ϸϸϸ

"In earth everyone come alone and go alone,
Accept this truth."

Pratibha Chaurel

ϸϸϸ

"Sometimes you don't want to support wrong things,
this is also the reason that people leave you alone."

Pratibha Chaurel

ϸϸϸ

"Not all time we support one person,
b'coz we are human being who knows,
what is the thing and who do right things."

Pratibha Chaurel

FIVE

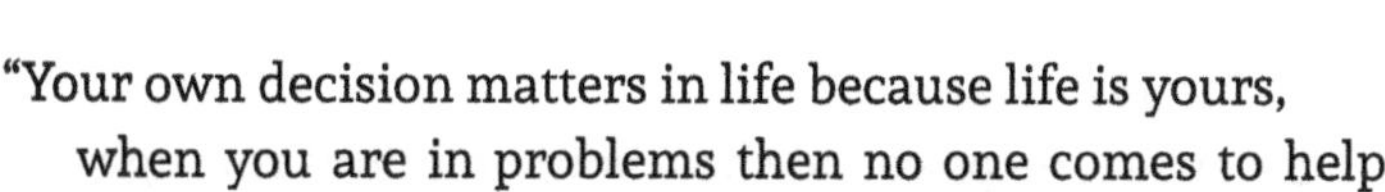

"Your own decision matters in life because life is yours,
when you are in problems then no one comes to help you,
so, help yourself."
Pratibha Chaurel

"Loneliness appeared when you don't accept it,
Loneliness disappeared when you accept it."
Pratibha Chaurel

"Understanding is better than argument."
Pratibha Chaurel

"Two learnings that are close to my hearts are:
Never give up
Take your own decisions."
Pratibha Chaurel

SIX

"Take interest in arts
because it helps you to show your emotions through sketches, drawings and paintings."
Pratibha Chaurel

"Currently there are two forms of social media
Make your life
Or
Ruin your life.
It depends on you how you use social media."
Pratibha Chaurel

"One fear that I still hold onto in life is don't trust blindly."
Pratibha Chaurel

"There is nothing more powerful than god,
So believe in god."
Pratibha Chaurel

SEVEN

“In our life we have so many dreams to fulfill but sometimes it’s very hard because we also have so many responsibilities to fulfill.”

Pratibha Chaurel

ꝒꝒꝒ

“Time never speak but still it teach you so many things.”

Pratibha Chaurel

ꝒꝒꝒ

“It is better to leave when No one is interested to listen you.”

Pratibha Chaurel

ꝒꝒꝒ

“Never lose hope either you see it or not,
b’coz we also not see sun in night,
but we know that on tomorrow sun will rise.”

Pratibha Chaurel

EIGHT

"In life it doesn't matter you succeed or not,

but if you are a responsible person then you are a great and loveable person."

Pratibha Chaurel

"The biggest adventures I have experienced in life is,

Love yourself and be yourself."

Pratibha Chaurel

"Never miss the opportunity the life gives you,

because not all time life gives you second chance."

Pratibha Chaurel

"All time waiting is not right thing sometimes take action."

Pratibha Chaurel

NINE

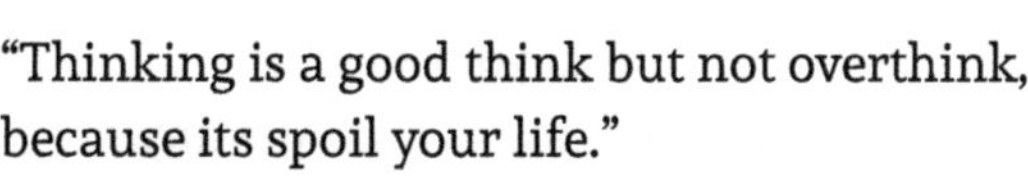

"Thinking is a good think but not overthink,
because its spoil your life."
Pratibha Chaurel

ꝑꝑꝑ

"Change yourself if you're bad person but
Don't change yourself if you know you are a good person."
Pratibha Chaurel

ꝑꝑꝑ

If you don't love animals
don't hurt them also,
earth is a place of animals also not only for humans.
Pratibha Chaurel

ꝑꝑꝑ

Always ready to close the door for those people, who are always ready to insult you and give you wrong advice.
Pratibha Chaurel

TEN

Life going to change according to your destiny,
Time going to change according to your destiny,
but
Change yourself according to your life and time,
It depends on you not on your destiny.
Pratibha Chaurel

Sometimes life is like a guitar,
If you know how to play it's awesome,
If you don't know how to play then it's worst,
also in life if you know how to live it's awesome,
and if you don't know how to live then it's worst.
Pratibha Chaurel

No matter how attractive human beauty is,
whenever you see the beauty of nature,
you think nothing is more beautiful than this god gifted nature.
Pratibha Chaurel

Don't waste your time to see others success,

Invest your time in learning and making yourself to grow and get succeed.

Pratibha Chaurel

ELEVEN

People think the person who is silent don't know anything,
but It's wrong, they know everything and understand all thing,
but still silent, b'coz they know that every people
have their own opinion.
Pratibha Chaurel

ꝒꝒꝒ

Don't be sad if your hard work not get success,
because you have experience and that is also a achievement of life.
Pratibha Chaurel

ꝒꝒꝒ

Happiness come from ourselves,
because if we don't want to be happy then there is no one who make us happy, so be happy yourself.
Pratibha Chaurel

ꝒꝒꝒ

No one gonna change your life except you,
so don't expect that someone
is coming and change your life,
because that never gonna happen,

so stand up and take actions.
Pratibha Chaurel

TWELVE

Make your own style,
Make your own way,
Because life is yours,
Live in your own way.
Pratibha Chaurel

Life is tough when you take it seriously,
so enjoy the life and take it easy.
Pratibha Chaurel

Keep helping people, no matter how much trouble there is in your life,
because instead of goodness,
you will definitely get its fruits somewhere.
Pratibha Chaurel

The reality of life is that you have to travel the journey of life alone,
so do not expect anything from anyone.
Except yourself.
Pratibha Chaurel

THIRTEEN

Don't sacrifice your dreams for someone's love,
because the one who really loves you will make your dreams come true.
Pratibha Chaurel

Do only as much as someone needs,
not exceeding the limit,
otherwise, they will get used to your work and if you ever refuse them,
then they started backbiting.
Pratibha Chaurel

Instead of looking for peace in others, seek within yourself,
Do that thing which makes you happy, you will find peace automatically.
but if you find peace in someone then you will get disappointment.
Pratibha Chaurel

Try till you are not dead,
Try till you have hope,

Try till you have energy,
Try till you live,
Try it, but never give up.
Pratibha Chaurel

FOURTEEN

Hear always about society,
Think always about society,
Stop thinking and hearing about society,
Do whatever you want to do,
because life is yours not societies.
Pratibha Chaurel

Victory and defeat are a matter of later,
But if we don't even try
then how we win.
Pratibha Chaurel

As the rising sun dispels the darkness,
the burning lamp removes the darkness,
In the same way the thinking of your mind,
Ends the darkness of life.
Pratibha Chaurel

Everyone's thinking is always wrong, it is not necessary,
Sometimes the way of showing and telling the story is also wrong.

Pratibha Chaurel

FIFTEEN

"Every relationship has its own value,
so don't compare anyone with anyone,
rather try to understand them."
Pratibha Chaurel

ᑭᑭᑭ

"The person who does not like to bow down again and again,
People like to bow down them again and again."
Pratibha Chaurel

ᑭᑭᑭ

"It is not always necessary to win in life,
but sometimes we should also be defeated,
so that we should not be proud of victory,
and instead of mourning the loss,
we should learn something from it and move forward."
Pratibha Chaurel

ᑭᑭᑭ

"If you judge the person without knowing them,
then anyone can do the same to you,
So it's better stop being judgemental. "
Pratibha Chaurel

SIXTEEN

"If something you do gives you a happiness then do it,
because your own happiness is also matters in your life."
Pratibha Chaurel

ღღღ

"If you want to give some happiness to someone, without asking them,
then also see whether they are happy with that or not,
because if they are not happy with the thing that you are giving them,
then
It's a burden not happiness."
Pratibha Chaurel

ღღღ

"Some things are right, but still people feel it's wrong,
because their way of seeing and understanding thing is wrong."
Pratibha Chaurel

ღღღ

"Follow your intuition always it doesn't matter what the situation is,
Because your intuition always shows you the right way."

Pratibha Chaurel

SEVENTEEN

"Money matters a lot today,
but give importance to relationships also,
because money doesn't work everywhere."
Pratibha Chaurel

ꝒꝒꝒ

"People always put love first,
but according to me,
First it will be someone goodness,
then, truth then respect then trust and then love,
because no one likes to be with a bad person,
No matter how much love and respect they give you."
Pratibha Chaurel

ꝒꝒꝒ

"Loyality is lacking more than love in today's world."
Pratibha Chaurel

ꝒꝒꝒ

"Sometimes life stands at such a point that we don't understand,
Whether we think about yourself or your loved ones."
Pratibha Chaurel

EIGHTEEN

"If you love, do it for a lifetime,

not to change it again and again, because it is not necessary that

everyone is like you, who likes to change the love,

there are some people in this world who love once and want to be with them in their whole life,

and do not want to change it."

Pratibha Chaurel

ÞÞÞ

"There is pain in everyone's life, the only difference is that not everyone cries, some people hide their pain behind laughter."

Pratibha Chaurel

ÞÞÞ

"Life is not always meant to walk and run it is also for rest,

So, when you don't understand something, take rest,

because you don't know that in future there will be a chance to take a rest or not."

Pratibha Chaurel

ÞÞÞ

"The desire of a person never ends,

They need something or the other,
Sometimes they need a house,
Sometimes they need money.
Sometimes they need love, and
When they gets everything,
Then they need peace."
Pratibha Chaurel

NINETEEN

"In today's world, there is a lack of loyalty more than love,

People have love but still they look others and attracted towards them, and in this affair they lost their love and regret later."

Pratibha Chaurel

ღღღ

"No one can know anyone well because every person has a side,

which they keeps hidden and this is also necessary for your their own safety."

Pratibha Chaurel

ღღღ

"The biggest drawback of a human being is that he/she does not want to give to anyone what he/she wants,

as if he/she wants people to take care of him/her,

but he/she himself does not take care

of anyone,

they love respect but himself does not like to give respect to anyone,

so what you can't do it for others,

you can't even expect from others."

Pratibha Chaurel

ꝒꝒꝒ

"Hope is a good thing but when you keep it from yourself not from others."

Pratibha Chaurel

ꝒꝒꝒ

"Somethings in life are not in our control,
so it is better to let them go,
don't Force them to be with you."
Pratibha Chaurel

TWENTY

“Work is very important in life but rest is also very important because

If you will not rest and remain unhealthy then how will you work.”

Pratibha Chaurel

ꝒꝒꝒ

“Balance is very important in life, because the person who is good in

balancing they can achieve anything in life.”

Pratibha Chaurel

ꝒꝒꝒ

“Some coincidence happen again and again in life,

that is not normal, they are because that showing us the way or

they trying to tell us something.”

Pratibha Chaurel

ꝒꝒꝒ

“Learn to trust your love because if the is raw then anyone will easily separate you from your love,

but if the trust is strong then no one would dare to do that.”

Pratibha Chaurel

♡♡♡

"It is very easy to love a good person but understanding the good qualities of that good person is very difficult."

Pratibha Chaurel

TWENTY-ONE

"No matter how much you do for someone, there will be always
complaint in his mind for you,
so, it's better to focus on yourself,
Not on people's complaints."
Pratibha Chaurel

ÞÞÞ

"Every relationship has its own value,
why do people compare,
only parents can give parental love,
brothers and sisters have their own values,
friends also have their own place,
love also has its own place,
We need everyone's love,
No one is more than anyone,
Everyone has their own role in life."
Pratibha Chaurel

ÞÞÞ

"If you ran away from loneliness you will get depression,
It is better to be friends with him, you will get peace."
Pratibha Chaurel

ÞÞÞ

“While walking in the path of dreams, there always comes a time when we are completely broken, no way is visible,

and that time we also understand how to be strong and how to be patient to make our dreams come true.”

Pratibha Chaurel

TWENTY-TWO

"Trust in yourself and your god the destination will come automatically."

Pratibha Chaurel

"There are some people in this world who themselves do not listen to anyone and expect others to listen and understand them."

Pratibha Chaurel

"If someone does not respect and love you,

It does not mean that you don't deserve that thing, the thing is that,

you are placing hope from wrong person."

Pratibha Chaurel

"They are some people in this world who do bad deeds themselves and cry and react like they have not done anything."

Pratibha Chaurel

TWENTY-THREE

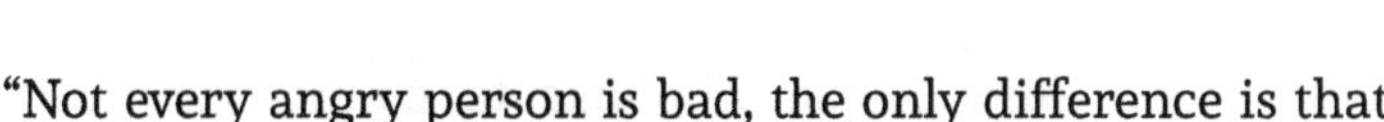

"Not every angry person is bad, the only difference is that they cannot see wrong and bad things, so they get angry."
Pratibha Chaurel

"Everyone teaches us from childhood that speak the truth,
but the reality is that whenever we speak the truth,
no one wants to hear."
Pratibha Chaurel

"If you want to fulfill your dreams, then do not say much because
people believe when they see not when you speak."
Pratibha Chaurel

"Respect every relationship but keep this thing from both the sides not only from one side."
Pratibha Chaurel

TWENTY-FOUR

"Stay away from people who like to count everything because such people helpless, and pretend more."

Pratibha Chaurel

ꝒꝒꝒ

"Everything in this world is related to appearances somewhere,

but if is related to someone's happiness then definitely do it."

Pratibha Chaurel

ꝒꝒꝒ

"When you live with someone then also think about them,

Not only about yourself for what you like and what makes you happy,

because if you do not care about the happiness of the other person,

then there is no point in being with them.

So don't spoil their whole life by staying with them,

It's better to be alone for the rest of your life."

Pratibha Chaurel

ꝒꝒꝒ

"To get any good thing, it is not only necessary to love them, you have to be equally good so that you became worthy of getting them."

Pratibha Chaurel

TWENTY-FIVE

"To get any good thing, it is not only necessary to love them,
you have to be equally good so that you became worthy of getting them."
Pratibha Chaurel

"Life is too short to do evil to anyone,
It is better to do some work, not to defame anyone."
Pratibha Chaurel

"It is not necessary that there is always a reason to like everything in life,
sometimes we like some things which we have no reason to like,
But still, we like them very much."
Pratibha Chaurel

"If a person is making fun of you again and again,
then stop them because your silence will make fun of you for life and then later you will be sick and you will be hurt,

it is better that you stop him earlier so that they know their boundaries."

Pratibha Chaurel

TWENTY-SIX

"While motivating others,

sometimes we get so demotivated that we do not know what to do next,

but people do not understand this because they think that we will handle everything in our life.

While it does not happen every time."

Pratibha Chaurel

"Never let anyone down so much that seeing their height you can't even make eye contact with them and then you yourself regret what you did before."

Pratibha Chaurel

" The place where we are born is the fate given by God, but if we stay there for the rest of our life, then it is our destiny, not the fate given by God."

Pratibha Chaurel

"In today's world it is more difficult to survive a good person than a bad person."

Pratibha Chaurel

TWENTY-SEVEN

"No matter how many rights you give to someone in your life, a boundary is needed so that they knows what is there limits."

Pratibha Chaurel

"Why do you want that every person understands you, if this happens then anyone can take advantage of you at any time, so it is better that you do not try to explain to anyone about yourself, tell only as much as is needed."

Pratibha Chaurel

"It is not a big deal to love someone, one should also know to appreciate him, it is better to learn to appreciate someone along with love."

Pratibha Chaurel

"Keep trying in life, who knows whether you will win or not, but you will definitely get experience and the same experience will take you forward and will win one day."

Pratibha Chaurel

TWENTY-EIGHT

"Karma is not a joke but a reality, whether you do good or bad, you will have to pay its price along with interest in the coming time, so it is better to do good, not bad."

Pratibha Chaurel

"Whether you like someone or not, but definitely respect him because your likes and dislikes do not prove that he/she is worthy of respect or not. So respect everyone."

Pratibha Chaurel

"Do you want someone to understand you then you try to be open up with them because they are also your kind of person who will understand only when you tell them about yourself not when you don't, because they are also human not a god who can Understand you without telling."

Pratibha Chaurel

"There is definitely a chapter in the life of every person, which has given him a lot of pain, but from the same pain, they learned how to live and fight in life, so it is better not to cry after remembering that pain. Rather, think that from there you have learned to live in life strongly."

Pratibha Chaurel

TWENTY-NINE

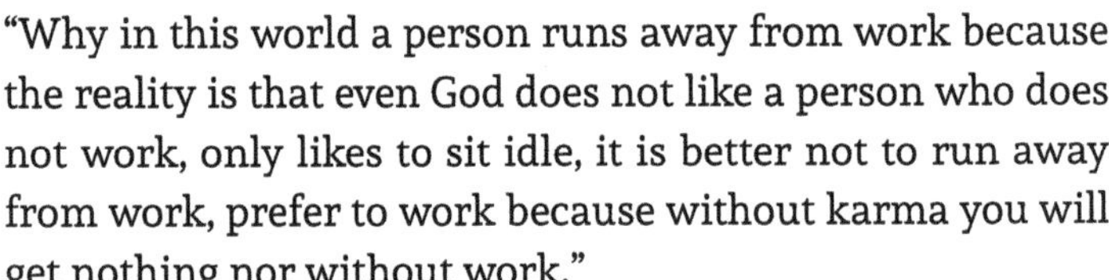

"Why in this world a person runs away from work because the reality is that even God does not like a person who does not work, only likes to sit idle, it is better not to run away from work, prefer to work because without karma you will get nothing nor without work."

Pratibha Chaurel

"That no matter how much you try to get something in life, there will definitely be something that will be missed, better do not regret what you miss and keep what you get with love."

Pratibha Chaurel

"There is defeat in life when you say that it will not happen to me now not when you get defeat from somewhere."

Pratibha Chaurel

" Timing of everything changes in life, its place changes if today someone is humiliating you by thinking of you that you are not worthy so just forgive them and move on, Because tomorrow your time will also come, then they will automatically know your ability, they stop you b'coz they don't want you to be win, so don't waste your time by being sad about their talk, move forward and win."

Pratibha Chaurel

9 798886 840360

Printed by Libri Plureos GmbH in Hamburg,
Germany